PUT YOUR Words TO Work

A 31-DAY FAITH PROJECT

Gloria Copeland

Put Your Words to Work: A 31-Day Faith Project

ISBN 978-1-60463-263-7   21-0035

22 21 20 19 18 17   6 5 4 3 2 1

© 2017 Gloria Copeland

Kenneth Copeland Publications
Fort Worth, TX 76192-0001

For more information about Kenneth Copeland Ministries, visit kcm.org or call 1-800-600-7395 (U.S. only) or +1-817-852-6000.

Table of Contents

*I*ntroduction—31 Days to Changing Your Life!. 7

*D*AY 1
Words Are Power Containers. 11

*D*AY 2
God's Words Are Life. 17

*D*AY 3
The Word Talks to You. 23

*D*AY 4
Say What You Want!. 29

*D*AY 5
Get Out of My Garden! 35

*D*AY 6
What Are You Saying About Others? .41

*D*AY 7
No Deposit—No Return 47

*D*AY 8
Change What You're Hearing. 53

*D*AY 9
Speak Love. 59

$\mathcal{D}$AY 10
Talk, Talk, Talk 65

$\mathcal{D}$AY 11
Your Future Is Bright! 71

$\mathcal{D}$AY 12
Take a Crash Course 77

$\mathcal{D}$AY 13
Speak Forth His Praises 83

$\mathcal{D}$AY 14
You've Got to *Say* Something 89

$\mathcal{D}$AY 15
You Really Don't Have to Cuss 95

$\mathcal{D}$AY 16
Give the Holy Spirit Something to Help 101

$\mathcal{D}$AY 17
Go Ahead! Paddle Upstream 107

$\mathcal{D}$AY 18
Speak Your Healing 113

$\mathcal{D}$AY 19
Speak His Words About Yourself .119

$\mathcal{D}$AY 20
The Trap of Flattering Words 125

$\mathcal{D}$AY 21
You're Doing Great—Don't Quit .131

DAY 22
Keep Your Words in Line 137

DAY 23
Talk to Yourself! 143

DAY 24
Answer Your Circumstances With Joy! 149

DAY 25
Protect Your Spirit With Your Mouth 155

DAY 26
Shout the Victory! 161

DAY 27
There's a Miracle in Your Mouth 167

DAY 28
The Price of Compromise 173

DAY 29
Speak His Words Day and Night 179

DAY 30
Give Yourself a New Name 185

DAY 31
In the Long Run... 191

How's Your Habit? 197

Renew Your Mind...and Your Mouth!
Scriptures to Live By... 199

Introduction

31 DAYS TO CHANGING YOUR LIFE!

When Ken and I turned our words around, we turned our lives around. But we didn't turn our mouths around until we filled our hearts with God's Word.

That was more than 45 years ago, and we're still filling our hearts with God's Word and speaking it out of our mouths. It's a principle from God's Word that will never change.

When we turned our mouths around, Ken was just getting started in ministry. We couldn't afford for me to go with him to meetings, so I was home with our children. I didn't have any money to spend, so I didn't go shopping. I didn't have any real distractions, so when I wasn't taking care of the house (think *small* house!) and the children, I was in the Word. I listened to reel-to-reel tapes and took notes—so many that I almost wrote down entire tapes! I was in revival all by myself. When Ken would call home, I'd just preach to him, and he'd preach to me.

One day, as I sat there listening to a tape by Kenneth E. Hagin, he referenced Mark 11:23 saying, "That whosoever shall say unto this mountain, Be thou removed, and be thou cast into the sea; and shall not doubt in his heart, but shall believe that those things which he saith shall come to pass; he shall have whatsoever he saith" *(King James Version)*. Instantly, I saw what the Lord was saying.

He spoke to me: *In consistency lies the power.* The scripture said, "but shall believe that those things which he saith." The key was not the thing a person says as a single request, but those things he *continually* says.

When Ken called home the next time, I started preaching. He had seen it in the Word as well. We saw that our words were bringing to pass in our lives what we had right then. We saw that if we wanted to change our lives—change the lack, change our finances, change our home—we would have to change our words and start saying continually what God's Word says about us and our situation.

That was so long ago, but it has been the key to our walking in the faith of God all these years.

In the consistency of speaking right words lies the power of God to deliver you. Your words, based on God's Word, open the door to abundant life. That was the revelation God was speaking to me, and He's speaking it to you today.

If you want a change in your life, you have to make a change. Changing your words is the best place to start. What you and I say day in and day out is what will come to pass in our lives. We have to set ourselves to speak words that are of God, that are what we want to come to pass in our lives. To release faith, we have to have confidence that our words will come to pass.

When Ken and I realized this, we made some extreme changes. We agreed that we were no longer going to speak any words except those we wanted to come to pass. We agreed to quit talking about lack, defeat, sickness and disease. And we started talking the Word of God regarding healing, abundance and well-being. *We chose to talk faith words,* and our lives turned around. We could see change instantly. It took us 11 months to get out of debt. We could see improvement as soon as we turned our mouths around.

We had to work at it and help each other. If one of us said something we didn't want to come to pass, the other one would say, "That's your confession and I'm in agreement with it." We did that to help each other hear what we were carelessly saying. That sounds extreme, but it really helped us change what we were speaking. It made us conscious of what was coming out of our mouths.

As believers we are to live our spiritual lives on the offensive side, not on the defensive side. We shouldn't be just reacting to what the devil does, we should be applying pressure on him by obeying the Word, walking in faith, and speaking right words out of our mouths.

For you to succeed in life, the Word has to be in two places, in your heart and in your mouth. The Word that is alive in you is the Word that talks to you. When you're in a hard place, what's inside you is what will come out. If you've put the Word in there, it will come out of your mouth and deliver you.

This book is designed to help you turn your mouth around. It's designed to help you renew your mind—and consequently your mouth—to speak the power of God into your life...to speak what you really want to come to pass.

I've heard it takes practicing something 21 days to make a habit. Well, I'm giving you 31. By reading and meditating on each day's message in this book, you can change the wrong habits you have developed of speaking wrong words—and the Lord will help you!

If you get to the end of 31 days and you're still having trouble keeping your words in line, just start over. Read and re-read every day until your mouth is speaking God's words of life, abundance, health, joy, prosperity, faith, promotion, peace and everything else you really want in your life.

The bottom line is, if you'll keep your words obedient to God's Word, you'll come out on top every time.

So get started. Make a commitment to yourself and to God to read each day's message and act on it, and in 31 days, I believe your life will be changed for the better!

Gloria Copeland

DAY 1

Words Are Power Containers

"Death and life are in the power of the tongue, and they
who indulge in it shall eat the fruit of it [for death or life]."

Proverbs 18:21, The Amplified Bible, Classic Edition

The power of God's Word has a profound effect on our lives. But most believers don't really understand the degree to which this is true. They only realize that words convey information.

Words are far more powerful than that! They actually serve as containers for spiritual power. According to Proverbs 18:21, they have the ability to carry faith or fear, blessing or cursing, life or death.

People sometimes speak idle or empty words, but God never does. Every word He has ever spoken has been filled with faith, power and life. In fact, God's Word actually contains within it the power to bring itself to pass. For example, in Isaiah 55:11 He says, "My word...shall not return to Me void, but it shall accomplish what I please, and it shall prosper in the thing for which I sent it."

Every word of God is backed by His faith, and is as full of power today as it was the moment He said it. So when you believe the Word, and your faith comes together with His faith, the power of that Word is released. The Holy Spirit goes into action, and the Word explodes into this natural realm and becomes a reality in your life!

That's what happened when you were born again. You heard or read God's Word: "That if you confess with your mouth the Lord Jesus and believe in your heart that God has raised Him from the dead, you will be saved" (Romans 10:9). With words, you received Jesus as your Lord and Savior. You believed that Word, spoke it in faith, and the power of the Holy Spirit was released, transforming your dead, fallen spirit into a reborn spirit, re-created in the image of Jesus Himself.

Now, think about this a minute. If His Word can save you and give you eternal life, it can accomplish everything else you need: healing, finances, spiritual growth, a new job, a new home, a new car, restored relationships, a better marriage, whatever it is you need or desire *today*. You can speak words of life, blessing and truth *in faith,* and as vessels of God's power, they will begin to effect change in the spiritual realm. This will eventually manifest in the natural realm.

In other words, you have the power to effect change in your life by *speaking* with your mouth the words of peace and blessing that you believe in your heart, based on what God has already spoken.

And as you speak God's words, they begin to come to pass for you.

START THIS VERY FIRST DAY changing your world by changing your words. Every time you hear yourself say something like, "That just scares me to death," catch yourself. Shut the door to fear and begin to retrain yourself by confessing the truth based on 2 Timothy 1:7 and Psalm 118:17. Say instead: "I do not receive fear. I walk in faith. God has not given me a spirit of fear, therefore I cast it out of my life. God has given me a spirit of power, love and a sound mind. I let the peace of God rule in my life by the Word of God. I shall not die, but live, and declare the works of the Lord."

You can apply this same Bible truth if you hear yourself say, "That just drives me crazy!" You don't want to go crazy. No one does. But by saying that, you're creating an opportunity for that to come to pass in your life.

So correct yourself when you slip up and say careless words. Confess the truth, "God has not given me a spirit of fear, but of power, love and a sound mind!" Amen!

STEP OF FAITH:

What are you believing God for today? Think about any careless words you've spoken over that situation. Now repent for those words, and begin speaking faith-filled words from this point forward!

NOTES

NOTES

NOTES

DAY 2

GOD'S WORDS
ARE LIFE

*"The word of God is living and powerful, and sharper than any
two-edged sword, piercing even to the division of soul
and spirit, and of joints and marrow."*
Hebrews 4:12

You can spend a lifetime studying the Word like a textbook, just to gain natural knowledge, just to learn facts, and it won't generate faith or do anything else for you spiritually. For the Word to be effective in your life, you have to let it become more than just a book to you. You must treat it as though God is speaking to you personally through its pages. You must let God's words jump out of your Bible and into your heart, so they can abide and take up residence there. Receive God's Word as God speaking to you! Your new heart is a depository for God's Word.

God's words can dwell in you because they are not tired, dead, old phrases. They are supernatural, spiritual words that originated in heaven. As Hebrews 4:12 says:

> The Word that God speaks is alive and full of power [making it active, operative, energizing, and effective]; it is sharper than any two-edged sword, penetrating

to the dividing line of the breath of life (soul) and
[the immortal] spirit, and of joints and marrow [of the
deepest parts of our nature], exposing and sifting and
analyzing and judging the very thoughts and purposes
of the heart *(The Amplified Bible, Classic Edition)*.

God's words had life in them the moment He first spoke
them. He framed the world with His words. And even though they
have been written down in a Book for thousands of years, they
are still His words, powerful and full of life. His words are eternal.
Jesus said God's words are Spirit and they are life (John 6:63). So
when you take the words that are in the Bible and put them in
your heart and in your mouth, they have God's power in them to
bring themselves to pass.

God's Word makes a circle. It comes down to us from Him
like rain from heaven and goes into the soil of our hearts (Mark 4).
Then, we lift those words back up to Him in faith, and He brings
them to pass in our lives. Isaiah 55:10-11 says it like this:

As the rain and snow come down from the heavens,
and return not there again, but water the earth and
make it bring forth and sprout, that it may give seed
to the sower and bread to the eater, so shall My word
be that goes forth out of My mouth: it shall not return
to Me void [without producing any effect, useless] but
it shall accomplish that which I please and purpose,
and it shall prosper in the thing for which I sent it *(The
Amplified Bible, Classic Edition)*.

TAKE TIME TO MAKE DEPOSITS of His Word inside you. Then because you believe the Word God has spoken, start speaking. Speak words of peace into your life, healing to your body and increase to your finances. Speak love and blessing to your family.

Speak words of life to your co-workers and blessings on your day. Don't say, "Oh, it's Monday again!" Say, "Today is a great day. The Lord has made it. I rejoice and am glad in it!" (See Psalm 118:24.) "This is Marvelous Monday...Tremendous Tuesday...Wonderful Wednesday...Thanksgiving Thursday... Freedom Friday...Satisfied Saturday." And Super Sunday? Well, that's God's day. It has to be good!

STEP OF FAITH:

What words from God are you depositing in to your heart today? Write them down, and begin speaking them over yourself, your family and your co-workers. Then watch how situations you thought were impossible begin to change!

NOTES

NOTES

NOTES

DAY 3

THE WORD TALKS TO YOU

"My son, give attention to my words; incline your ear to my sayings. Do not let them depart from your eyes; keep them in the midst of your heart; for they are life to those who find them, and health to all their flesh. Keep your heart with all diligence, for out of it spring the issues of life."

Proverbs 4:20-23

If you want the Word to produce powerful results in your life, you can't be content just to know what it says. You must believe it, meditate on it and say it until it abides in you so that you will say it and obey it. (We call that acting on the Word.)

The secret to the Word abiding in you is to put the Word into your heart in abundance, so it will dwell and come alive in you! You must give your attention to it, just like God instructed Joshua to do:

> Turn not from it to the right hand or to the left, that you may prosper wherever you go. This Book...shall not depart out of your mouth, but you shall meditate on it day and night, that you may observe and do according to all that is written in it. For then you shall

make your way prosperous, and then you shall deal wisely and have good success (Joshua 1:7-8, *Amplified Bible, Classic Edition*).

I realize, of course, that you can't walk around reading your Bible 24 hours a day. But you can keep the Word *abiding* in you 24 hours a day.

Ken and I first learned to walk by faith back in the 1960s by listening to tapes by Kenneth E. Hagin. Back then we didn't have the convenience of technology that is available now. We had to use the big 7-inch reel-to-reel tapes.

In addition, whenever Kenneth E. Hagin held a meeting in Tulsa, we found a way to be there. As I recall, in the year we lived there, he held four 10-day meetings, and we didn't miss one of them. We had to slip and slide our way over ice-covered streets to attend some of them, but we did it because we were so hungry for the Word!

That hunger paid off, too. Before long, things in our lives began to change. Because we started abiding in the Word, the Word started abiding in us (John 15:7).

How do you know if the Word is abiding in you? It begins to speak to you. If the Word is not talking to you, then it's not alive in you and you need to take action!

The Word that's abiding in you, that's alive in you, is the Word that talks to you. It's the Word that leads you moment by moment as you go about your day. The abiding Word will come up in your heart, much like the words and notes of a familiar song might spontaneously run through your mind.

The Word that's in you in abundance is also the Word you hear coming out of your mouth, "for out of the abundance of the heart his mouth speaks" (Luke 6:45).

If you are in a situation where you need a scripture to come out of your mouth, but find yourself speaking doubt and fear instead, it's an indication that the Word needed to overcome the situation is not alive in you.

To conquer the challenges of the world, the flesh and the devil, you must have the spiritual strength within you that only the engrafted Word can provide. You have to be so established in that Word that it automatically rises up within you in a moment of crisis. You have to be like the young men the Apostle John wrote to saying, "...You are strong, and the word of God abides in you, and you have overcome the wicked one" (1 John 2:14).

So get into the Word. Allow it to rise up within you and *speak* to you...and then *you* speak it out. That's how you become more than a conqueror in Christ Jesus (Romans 8:37)!

PRACTICE THESE THINGS TODAY:

- If you're one of those people who says something like: "Yeah, my father and grandfather both had heart attacks. I probably won't ever see 40," instead begin saying, "I will live out the length of my days. My youth is renewed like the eagle's. I run and I am not weary. I walk and do not faint. I'm healthy and strong. My mouth is filled with good things" (Isaiah 40:31; Psalm 103:1-5).

- Or, if you say things like: "I don't know how we're going to pay the electric bill. It's so high!" Change your circumstances by saying in faith, "God is able to make all grace (every favor and earthly blessing) come to [me] in *abundance,* so that [I] may *always* and under *all circumstances* and whatever the need be self-sufficient [possessing enough to require no aid or support and furnished in abundance for every good work and charitable donation]" (2 Corinthians 9:8, *Amplified Bible, Classic Edition).*

Be sure to send us your testimony! We want to rejoice with you over God's goodness!

STEP OF FAITH:

What do you need? Find scriptures that apply to your situation and begin confessing them today. (See the scriptures in the back of this book for healing, finances, fear, relationships and more.)

NOTES

NOTES

DAY 4

SAY WHAT YOU WANT!

"If you live in Me [abide vitally united to Me] and My words remain in you and continue to live in your hearts, ask whatever you will, and it shall be done for you."

John 15:7, The Amplified Bible, Classic Edition

O ne reason it's so important to have the Word abiding in you in abundance is that when you come up against a test or a trial, Satan will put tremendous pressure on you to say negative things. You'll find yourself strongly tempted to speak the problem instead of the Word. But you can't do that and come out in victory.

In Mark 11:23, Jesus taught us that "whoever says...and does not doubt in his heart, but believes that those things he says will be done, he will have whatever he says." The realm of the spirit works in our lives according to *our* words. We have what we say. Our words are our faith speaking.

Satan knows that, so when pressure begins building in our circumstances, he pushes us to say what we have! He wants us to say, "I feel so sick!" instead of, "By Jesus' stripes I am healed." He wants us to say, "I'm broke!" instead of, "My God meets my needs according to His riches in glory."

Here's another illustration of this. Ken and I were in an elevator some time ago at a hotel. We stood in that elevator talking for a while, and soon realized we hadn't gone anywhere. Then it dawned on us that we'd pushed the button for the floor we were already on, instead of pushing the button for the floor we wanted. Pushing the button for the floor where we were didn't take us anywhere!

As believers, most of us do the same thing with our words. We say what we have instead of saying what we desire. As a result, things just stay the way they are. Even if we know we should be speaking the Word, when the pressure of adverse circumstances hits us, we won't be able to say what we should unless we're abiding in the Word, and the Word is abiding in us. Double up and give twice as much time and attention to the Word when the pressure is on!

WHATEVER SITUATIONS ARE IN YOUR LIFE today that you want to change, go to God's Word. Search out scriptures that you can stand on in prayer and speak them out all day long. Replace doubt words with His words—believing words.

For example, if you're having turmoil in your home, you can stand on and speak out Romans 15:13 and 2 Corinthians 13:11 throughout the day: "Lord, thank You that we are filled with all joy and peace that we may abound in hope. My household is of one mind and lives in peace. Amen!"

STEP OF FAITH:

Ask the Holy Spirit to point out to you when you say something contrary to God's Word. Then repent and begin saying only what God's Word says you can have in your life.

NOTES

NOTES

NOTES

DAY 5

GET OUT OF MY GARDEN!

"Put away from you false and dishonest speech, and willful
and contrary talk put far from you."
Proverbs 4:24, The Amplified Bible, Classic Edition

S atan is an outlaw. God has given us laws to keep him in line,
but he won't abide by them unless we enforce those laws.

That's not really surprising. Things work the same way
in the natural realm. In the United States, for example, we have
laws against murder, stealing and selling drugs. But if those laws
aren't enforced, what happens? Thieves and murderers continue
to operate. The law has to be enforced.

Once you understand that, you'll see why Satan works so
hard to get you to talk about your problems instead of God's
promises. He knows your authority to enforce God's law is in
your words. If he can get your words going in the wrong direc-
tion, he can get authority over your life—even though it doesn't
belong to him.

Satan doesn't care what belongs to him. He's a thief. He's a
killer. He takes what he can get. So you have to use the Word of
God on him when he tries to come into your garden and spoil it.

That's what Adam should have done when Satan showed up in *his* garden. The first time that creature opened his mouth to question the Word of God, Adam should have said, "Get out of my garden, you serpent!"

And that's what you and I should do, too. The first time the devil starts trying to bring doubt and unbelief to us, saying things like: "Do you really think God is going to heal you? Do you really think God cares about your marriage?" we should just tell him to take his lies and get out of our lives!

How do you do that? Just say, "Doubt, unbelief and fear, in the Name of Jesus, leave my presence." Remind yourself, "Yes, I really do believe the Word of God!" Quote the Word and don't stop. Refuse to listen to words that steal, kill and destroy (John 10:10).

Just keep on speaking and studying what the Word of God says about your situation until you're hearing that Word in your heart all day, instead of those lies of the devil. When you're walking in the authority God's given you and speaking the Word of God, then you'll have no trouble telling the devil, "Get out of my garden in the Name of Jesus!" And he has to flee (James 4:7).

WATCH YOUR WORDS carefully today. Remember this: The devil comes to get your words. Don't let him have them. It's up to you. Refuse to allow the devil into your garden through careless and foolish words. You have authority over your garden. It's your responsibility just as it was Adam's. For example, if you confess in exasperation, "I can't remember what to do! I'd forget my head if it weren't attached!" Stop! Change your confession and change your circumstances. Do the same thing Jesus did. When Satan came to tempt Him, Jesus answered him every time with, "It is written...."

Say in faith: "I *can* remember. Based on John 14:26, the Comforter, who is the Holy Spirit, teaches me all things, and brings all things to my remembrance. I walk in peace—the peace Jesus gave me. I refuse to allow my heart to be troubled, nor will I be afraid."

Then stand in faith. The Holy Spirit will show you what to do and what to say.

STEP OF FAITH:

What do you need the Holy Spirit to help you with today? Write it down. Speak the scriptures that support what you need. Be prepared so when the devil tries to tell you lies, you'll be armed and ready with a powerful Word from God.

NOTES

NOTES

NOTES

DAY 6

WHAT ARE YOU SAYING ABOUT OTHERS?

"The words of a whisperer or talebearer are as dainty morsels;
they go down into the innermost parts of the body."

Proverbs 18:8, The Amplified Bible, Classic Edition

S trife is one of the devil's deadliest weapons. James 3:16 says,
"For where envying and strife is, there is confusion and every evil work" *(King James Version).*

Satan uses strife to destroy churches, marriages, families and
companies. He uses any relationship that gives him opportunity to
get involved through strife. The definition of *strife* is "contention,
competition, fighting, quarreling, conflict." It's a stirring up of division and contention. Oh, and it can be subtle. It can start with an
offense or hurt, and then grow into bitterness. The next thing you
know, you're speaking strife and acting it out. You're gossiping
and talebearing to everyone who will listen. Strife is so opposite
to our commandment of love (John 13:34).

If you understand the danger of strife, and you've made a
commitment to keep it out of your life, you may have noticed
more pressure than ever to participate in it!

Maybe the devil has provoked someone to be rude to you

and hurt your feelings. Or maybe he made sure you found out about something someone else did wrong, and then you talked about it to others.

When he presents you with that opportunity, turn him down—*fast!* Treat that temptation to gossip and to stir up strife like you would a poisonous snake, because in the eyes of God, participating in strife is one of the most serious of sins. Proverbs 6:16-19 says, "These six things the Lord hates, indeed, seven are an abomination to Him: a proud look [the spirit that makes one overestimate himself and underestimate others], a lying tongue, and hands that shed innocent blood, a heart that manufactures wicked thoughts and plans, feet that are swift in running to evil, a false witness who breathes out lies [even under oath], and he who sows discord among his brethren" *(The Amplified Bible, Classic Edition).*

God considers stirring up strife such a severe sin that He lists it alongside murder and witchcraft (Galatians 5:19-21). So stay away from it. Ask God to reveal to you if you've entered into strife unintentionally. He may remind you of a time you passed along some gossip or criticized someone. If He does, repent, and be more conscious of those things in the future. Determine in your heart that from now on, if you see your brother sin, you'll believe God for him and pray for him, instead of perpetuating his problem by talking to everyone about it.

I realize sometimes that seems extremely difficult to do. But here's something that will help you. When you're tempted to get into strife by judging a fellow believer, remember Romans 14:4 and ask yourself, *Who are you to judge another's servant?...*

The devil will try to push you into making a decision about that person, to say whether he's guilty or not guilty. But don't give in to that pressure. It's not your job to judge others. (Isn't that a relief?) First Corinthians 4:5 says, "Therefore judge nothing before the time, until the Lord comes, who will both bring to light the hidden things of darkness and reveal the counsels of the hearts. Then each one's praise will come from God." If you're in a church where the pastor has done wrong, and you feel you don't want to follow him, that's fine. I don't blame you. Leave that church and go to one with a pastor you can trust and respect. But do it quietly. Don't sow discord with your mouth before you go. Most important of all, wherever you go, always be sure to leave in love, and guard diligently against strife. When you do, you will keep your faith strong and your blessings out of the devil's hands. Walk in love and you will always live in victory!

STEP OF FAITH:

If you've been offended by someone or have been in strife, repent right now and get into forgiveness and love so that the Word and the Holy Spirit will operate in full capacity in your life. Don't let strife hold you back from THE BLESSING of God!

NOTES

NOTES

NOTES

DAY 7

NO DEPOSIT—
NO RETURN

"How can you, being evil, speak good things? For out of the abundance of the heart the mouth speaks. A good man out of the good treasure of his heart brings forth good things, and an evil man out of the evil treasure brings forth evil things."

Matthew 12:34-35

I f the Word is not abiding in you as it should, if it's not coming up inside you when you need it, the solution is simple: Spend more time in it. Put more of the Word in your heart, and more will come out!

In some ways, your heart is like a bank account. If you want to make faith withdrawals on that account, you must have plenty of Word in there to back them. Jesus said, "A good man out of the good treasure of his heart brings forth good" (Luke 6:45). Or, as Matthew 12:33-35 says in the *New International Version:*

> Make a tree good and its fruit will be good, or make a tree bad and its fruit will be bad, for a tree is recognized by its fruit. You brood of vipers, how can you who are evil say anything good? For the mouth speaks

what the heart is full of. A good man brings good things out of the good stored up in him, and an evil man brings evil things out of the evil stored up in him.

If you haven't put money *in* the bank, when you write a check, money will not come *out* of the bank. The Word is the same way. If you haven't deposited God's Word about healing in your heart, for example, when sickness tries to come on you, words of healing will not come out of your mouth to resist it. Or, if you haven't deposited God's Word about prosperity in your heart, when the devil attacks your finances, you won't have the spiritual funds to fight back.

"But I did deposit God's Word about healing in my heart," you say. "I read healing scriptures every day back in 2008."

You probably deposited a thousand dollars in the bank a few years ago, too, but are you living on that money today? Not if you cashed checks on it and used it all.

By the same token, because you need to live by faith in this life, you are making withdrawals on your faith. The Word you put inside you is made strength and produces faith (if you believe it and obey it), and you're continually drawing on that supply of strength to meet the challenges that come your way. You will always encounter situations that require supernatural help.

So to keep your strength account from running low, you must continually make deposits of the Word. You should keep a fresh deposit of the Word in your heart at all times by putting it in every day. Then when your boss snaps at you, or your kids push you to the limit, you will be able to speak words of kindness, life and encouragement—instead of reacting with words from your flesh that stir up strife, discontent and resentment.

Give yourself an assignment today. Decide now, before you

go out the door, that today you will speak out the living Word that's on the inside of you. Decide now that you will respond in love and with a mouth that speaks forth the Word of God. You *can* do it!

STEP OF FAITH:

Ask the Holy Spirit to help you speak kind, loving and helpful words to everyone you come in contact with today.

NOTES

NOTES

NOTES

DAY 8

CHANGE WHAT YOU'RE HEARING

"This Book of the Law shall not depart out of your mouth."
Joshua 1:8, The Amplified Bible, Classic Edition

Have you ever been frustrated with yourself because of what you hear coming out of your mouth? Jesus said that out of the abundance of the heart, the mouth speaks (Luke 6:45). If you're focusing most of your attention on natural things—watching secular television, going to the movies, thinking about worldly matters, worrying about your job and family—then that's what you're going to talk about.

What you need to do is refocus your attention. Turn your attention toward God's Word, and keep it there.

In everyday terms, Joshua 1:8 says, "Talk the Word."

When I say talk the Word, I don't mean just every now and then when you're feeling spiritual. I mean continually. In Deuteronomy 6:7, God said you should talk His Word "when you sit at home and when you walk along the road, when you lie down and when you get up" *(New International Version)*.

That's pretty much all the time, isn't it? At home, at work, in the grocery store—wherever you are, keep the Word of God in your mouth.

Romans 10:17 tells us that "faith comes by hearing, and hearing by the word of God." So when you're continually speaking what God says, what He'll do, and what His promises are, you're going to be growing in faith because you're hearing the Word from yourself all the time.

Isn't that exciting? You can change what you're hearing. So start today. Fill your heart with an abundance of the Word and listen as your mouth gets in line with what God says about you, your life and circumstances.

STEP OF FAITH:

Think about the time you spend in leisurely activities. What amount of that time could you add to your time in the Word? Do it and watch how it pays off!

NOTES

NOTES

NOTES

DAY 9

SPEAK LOVE

"A gentle tongue [with its healing power] is a tree of life, but willful contrariness in it breaks down the spirit."

Proverbs 15:4, The Amplified Bible, Classic Edition

"Be ordering your behavior within the sphere of love, even as Christ also loved you and gave himself up in our behalf and in our stead as an offering and a sacrifice to God for an aroma of a sweet smell" (Ephesians 5:2, *Wuest Translation*).

There's no question about it, if you are a born-again believer, you want to walk in love. You can't help it; it's part of your new nature. But wanting to do it isn't enough. You have to go a step further and make a quality decision to *do* it!

Make up your mind in advance to obey the instruction in Ephesians 5:2 and constantly order your behavior—including your speech—within the *sphere of love*. Notice I said *in advance*. If you wait until you're facing a tough situation to decide how you want to respond, you'll almost certainly make the wrong choice.

So prepare yourself now for what's ahead. If there's a person in your life who is particularly difficult to love, make that person a special project—especially if he or she lives in the same house-hold with you! (This kind of person usually needs love even more than anyone else.) Make plans to not just "put up with him or her," but to go out of your way to be kind and loving.

"But Gloria," you may say, "you just don't know this person like I do. It would be too hard to love this person. I can't do it."

Yes, you can! You're a disciple of the Lord Jesus Christ. You are filled with His Holy Spirit and power. And God has planted in your heart His very own love—the love that never fails. So make a decision to give yourself over to that love, and let it flow.

Then start strengthening your spirit by feeding on what the Word of God says about love. As you meditate on that Word, it will energize and create within you the power and desire to will and to work for God's good pleasure. It will increase your ability to walk and talk in love.

Keep yourself on a steady diet of God's Word. Counteract the worldly voices and fleshly desires that pull you away from love by filling your ears and eyes with scriptures like 1 Corinthians 13. Read them at night before you go to bed. Read them in the morning when you wake up. Write them out on notecards and tape them to your bathroom mirror so you can meditate on them while you're brushing your teeth.

If you do that, I guarantee you, that Word will come alive in you. It will talk to you and help you stick with your decision to walk in love. When you get fed up with someone and you're about to tell him or her off, the Word will speak up and remind you that love is not touchy, fretful or resentful.

Then, instead of giving that person a piece of your mind, you'll give him the love of God, and he'll be blessed. God will be pleased, and you'll have the victory!

STEP OF FAITH:

Think about that person who is your "special project" right now. Look up verses on which you can begin meditating and speaking over him or her in prayer. As you do this consistently, you'll begin to speak it out to them in different ways. You'll speak and walk in love!

NOTES

NOTES

NOTES

DAY 10

TALK, TALK, TALK

"The words of a [discreet and wise] man's mouth are like deep waters [plenteous and difficult to fathom], and the fountain of skillful and godly Wisdom is like a gushing stream [sparkling, fresh, pure, and life-giving]."

Proverbs 18:4, The Amplified Bible, Classic Edition

Satan is like a salesman. He makes a presentation to you and tries to sell you a bill of goods. He tells you God doesn't really love you or that the Word won't work this time. He tells you that you don't have the strength to go on, or he'll even try to sell you on the idea that it would be easier for you just to curl up and die than to see this trial through in faith.

All he does is talk...talk...talk and lie...lie...lie. But you don't have to listen.

Now that talk can get very annoying, but remember, that's all he can do! He doesn't have any real power or authority over you. He can't make you talk his lies, but he'll surely try.

According to 1 Peter 5:8, he walks around as a roaring lion, "seeking whom he may devour." It doesn't say he *is* a lion. He just acts like one. Therefore, he can't devour you unless you let him.

Verse 9 says we are to resist the devil steadfastly. That means you have to use patience to resist him. He is, after all, a persistent fellow. He may pester you a thousand times a day, but if you'll resist him every time, he will flee from you every time (James 4:7).

First Corinthians 2:6 says that Satan and all the low-level demons he sends to aggravate you are "coming to nothing." Jesus stripped them of all their power and authority and left them with no power. Colossians 2:15 tells us, "[Jesus] spoiled principalities and powers, he made a show of them openly, triumphing over them in it" *(King James Version).*

The next time Satan starts his sales pitch, *talk back.* Continually remind yourself of who you are in Christ Jesus. Say, "I am a new creature in Christ Jesus. I am born of God. I am filled with the Holy Spirit who proceeds from the Father. I am endowed with the Name of Jesus, which is 'far above all principality and power and might and dominion, and every name that is named, not only in this age but also in that which is to come!' (Ephesians 1:21). He who is in me is greater than he who is in the world" (1 John 4:4).

Say, "Satan, I resist you in the Name of Jesus. Get out!" According to the Word of God in James 4:7, he will flee from you. He has to bow his knee to the Name of Jesus uttered in faith (Philippians 2:10-11)!

STEP OF FAITH: SPEAK THE WORD!

What lies has the devil been telling you? What are you going to say the next time he starts talking? Write it down— be prepared to run the enemy off with the Word of God.

NOTES

NOTES

NOTES

DAY 11

YOUR FUTURE IS BRIGHT!

"He who guards his mouth keeps his life, but he who opens wide his lips comes to ruin."

Proverbs 13:3, The Amplified Bible, Classic Edition

Your future is stored up in your heart. It's not dictated by your past, or your current circumstances. Your future is determined by you!

"Out of the abundance of the heart the mouth speaks. A good man out of the good treasure of his heart brings forth good things, and an evil man out of the evil treasure brings forth evil things" (Matthew 12:34-35).

In this verse, Jesus said that what is in your heart is what comes out of your mouth. So consider this: Who stored up the evil things that were in the evil man's heart? Obviously, the man himself did it. Who stored up the good things in the good man's heart? Again, the man himself did.

In the same way, you're the only one who can make deposits of God's Word into your heart. Your spouse can't do it for you. Your pastor can't do it for you. Even God can't do it for you.

God has already done His part to help you. He's the One who

made your heart a depository for His Word. He's the One who opened the account for you when you were born again. As the Scripture says, "God has dealt to each one a measure of faith" (Romans 12:3). The moment you were born again, He put the initial measure of faith in your heart—but you are the only one who can develop it.

And you can do that by putting the Word of God before your eyes and in your heart. Each time you make a deposit of the Word, your faith balance grows, and your future gets brighter. And there is no limit to the size of the deposits you can make!

The more you deposit, the better things are, because that's where you will draw from to change the circumstances in your life. For example, your heart holds the faith you'll need to cover any test or trial the devil tries to send your way. If you've just lost your job, for example, you can draw from the Word of God about His plans for your welfare and have peace that you can make it just fine. Your future really is bright! The Lord says in Jeremiah 29:11, "For I know the plans I have for you...plans to prosper you and not to harm you, plans to give you hope and a future" *(New International Version)*.

STEP OF FAITH:

Whatever you've been worrying about, speak to it right now. Don't speak the thoughts you've been thinking, but rather what the Word has to say about the object of your worry. Every time you're tempted to worry, or you catch yourself actually worrying, *speak* the desired end result. For example, if you're worrying about what your boss thinks about you, or how secure your job is, confess the Word concerning these things. Say, "Father, Your favor surrounds me like a shield. Psalm 5:12 says so. I thank You that I have favor with everyone I meet today, especially my boss. I thank You that my security is in You, not in what I see or feel with my natural senses."

Now, you've opened the door to making a difference. Now, things can start turning around!

NOTES

NOTES

NOTES

DAY 12

TAKE A CRASH COURSE

"Do not be conformed to this world, but be transformed by the renewing of your mind, that you may prove what is that good and acceptable and perfect will of God."

Romans 12:2

I f you're just getting started in the things of God, you may be wondering exactly how you "jump into faith." It's simple. Romans 10:17 says faith comes by hearing, and hearing by the Word of God.

When Ken and I first learned about the life of faith, we were so hungry for it that we took a crash course in the Word of God. Day and night, we listened to messages of the Word being preached.

In fact, for the biggest part of that first year, we hardly did anything but read, study and listen to the Word of God. We were so tired of being failures that we weren't interested in anything else but the Word of God. Ken was traveling at the time, and I was staying home with the children. But I was having revival all by myself!

I was in my own little world of God's Word and faith. I spent my extra time in the Word and listening to tapes. One day, I was hanging clothes on the line to dry, thinking about what I'd been learning, when the telephone rang. I ran inside to answer it but I was so caught up in my excitement about the Word, that instead of saying "Hello," I accidentally said, "Hallelujah!" My well was overflowing.

You may think that's extreme—but I recommend being extreme. I recommend you so saturate yourself with the Word of God there's no room in your thinking for unbelief, doubt and fear. Saturate your heart with the Word until it naturally begins to flow out of your mouth. Let it completely take over and renew your mind.

Then, when Satan lies to you and tells you that God is not listening to your prayers, that you won't receive your healing or get that new job, don't listen to him. Rebuke him in Jesus' Name. Remind yourself of the goodness of God. Say, "The Lord is good to all. He's full of compassion. His tender mercy is over all His works—and that includes me! I'm one of God's favorites!"

IF YOU'VE BEEN AFRAID to come to God with your needs, afraid to speak forth His Word for your life or afraid to expect His BLESSING to come your way, start meditating on His mercy today. Spend some time thinking about the ocean of goodness He's longing to pour into your life. Then open the door of faith and let it in! Be bold. Speak forth His Word for your life. Speak who you are in Christ Jesus and what belongs to you:

"I am a new creation" (2 Corinthians 5:17).

"I am the righteousness of God" (Romans 4).

"I am an overcomer by the blood of the Lamb and the word of my testimony" (Revelation 12:11).

"I am highly favored of God" (Proverbs 8:35).

"I am more than a conqueror" (Romans 8:37).

"All my needs are met in Christ Jesus according to His riches in glory," (Philippians 4:19)

...and so on.

Take a crash course in God's Word, and let THE BLESSING flow until you've reached the limit of your expectations. Then expect more. Experience the good life God has prepared for you. Speak it forth right now!

STEP OF FAITH:

Take a one-day crash course in faith. Write these scriptures out on cards or put them into your most used electronic device. Keep them in front of you all day. Put them before your eyes and in your ears. Confess them over and over, and begin expecting THE BLESSING of God to flow in every area of your life!

NOTES

NOTES

NOTES

DAY 13

SPEAK FORTH HIS PRAISES

"I will speak of Your testimonies also before kings, and will not be ashamed."

Psalm 119:46

J oy and praise release strength inside you and power on the outside. Psalm 22:3 says God inhabits our praises. When God's presence begins to come into our midst, our enemies fall back. They can't stand the presence of God.

Psalm 68:1-3 says,

> Let God arise, let His enemies be scattered; let those also who hate Him flee before Him. As smoke is driven away, so drive them away; as wax melts before the fire, so let the wicked perish at the presence of God. But let the righteous be glad; let them rejoice before God; yes, let them rejoice exceedingly.

Now, that's power! When you rise up in praise and worship and celebrate the victories of God, your enemies are scattered.

No wonder Satan has tried so hard to get God's people to sit still and be quiet. No wonder he has bound us up with traditions that taught us to sit back in "dignified" silence. For most of us, our traditions have taught us to *not* do the very things the Bible says we *are* to do when we worship and praise.

But tradition's day is over. I'm telling you, when the Spirit begins to move, inhibition has to flee. Zechariah 10:7 says, "[They] shall be like a mighty man, and their heart shall rejoice as if with wine."

You know what happens when people drink wine—they lose their inhibitions! That's what happened to the disciples on the Day of Pentecost. They had been hiding out only a few days before, but when the new wine of the Holy Spirit came upon them, suddenly they were on the streets acting so wild, everyone thought they had been drinking.

Listen, what God considers "dignified" and what you consider "dignified" are two different things. God wants you free. He doesn't want you bound up with traditions or fear of what other people might think.

He wants you to be free to laugh. He wants you to be free to leap and praise and sing. He wants you to be free to rejoice. He wants you to be free to *speak* forth His praises. He wants you so free that other people want what you have!

STEP OF FAITH:

Start speaking the praises of God today. As you commute to work or drive your children to school, start confessing verses from the Psalms together. Here's a few to help you get started:

> Psalm 9:1-3—"I will praise You, O Lord, with my whole heart; I will tell of all Your marvelous works. I will be glad and rejoice in You; I will sing praise to Your name, O Most High. When my enemies turn back, they shall fall and perish at Your presence."

> Psalm 34:1-3—"I will bless the Lord at all times; His praise shall continually be in my mouth. My soul shall make its boast in the Lord; the humble shall hear of it and be glad. Oh, magnify the Lord with me, and let us exalt His name together."

> Psalm 103:1-5—"Bless the Lord, O my soul; and all that is within me, bless His holy name! Bless the Lord, O my soul, and forget not all His benefits: Who forgives all your iniquities, who heals all your diseases, who redeems your life from destruction, who crowns you with lovingkindness and tender mercies, who satisfies your mouth with good things, so that your youth is renewed like the eagle's."

God inhabits the praises of His people!

NOTES

NOTES

NOTES

DAY 14

YOU'VE GOT TO *SAY* SOMETHING

"I believed and therefore I spoke."

2 Corinthians 4:13

C onsider the following scenario:

"Where do you want to go eat, honey?" the husband asks.

"Oh, I don't care. Anywhere you want to go is fine with me," she answers.

Taking his wife at her word, the husband goes to his favorite restaurant. The problem is, the wife doesn't really like his favorite restaurant. Once they get there and start to order, she's not so happy.

"What's wrong?"

"Oh, nothing," snaps the wife.

"Something is bothering you. What is it?"

"I didn't want to eat here. I want to eat somewhere else."

"Well, why didn't you say something?" he asks in exasperation.

That's just a small example, but it illustrates a very solemn truth. Someday, when our earthly lives are finished and we stand before Jesus, someone might say, "Lord, I really needed clothes for my children when I was on earth...I really needed healing for my body...I really needed deliverance from my circumstances."

I can just hear Jesus saying to us just what the husband said to his wife, "Well, why didn't you *say* something?!"

Those words may shock you. You may be sitting around in the midst of a crisis, waiting for God to act—when all the time, He's waiting for you. Jesus is waiting for each of us to take the power and dominion He gave us and use it to put those devil-generated crises where they belong—under our feet!

Jesus said, "I have been given all authority in heaven and on earth. Therefore, [you] go..." (Matthew 28:18-19, *New Living Translation*). You lay hands on the sick and they'll recover. You cast out the devil. In other words, Jesus was saying, "I'm giving you My authority, so use it!"

Whatever crisis you're facing right now, stand up, take authority over the devil and say something! Say, "Satan, in the Name of Jesus, I take authority over you and your assignment against me and my family. I take authority over you in this situation, and I declare deliverance and victory in the Name of Jesus! You take your hands off me. I am a child of the living God. I am covered by the blood of Jesus. And I am delivered! Amen."

Now, the key is to leave that place where you made your stand of faith and *keep saying* what you believed when you prayed—what you want to come to pass (Mark 11:23-24).

If you want a change, why don't you *say* what you want? Jesus said you can have what you say (verse 23)!

STEP OF FAITH:

What have you been hoping for but haven't asked for? Ask your heavenly Father—He is waiting for you to ask so He can bless you. Start believing it today, and don't stop saying and believing until you have it!

NOTES

NOTES

NOTES

DAY 15

YOU REALLY DON'T HAVE TO CUSS

"Let no corrupt word proceed out of your mouth, but what is good for necessary edification, that it may impart grace to the hearers."

Ephesians 4:29

W hat we say with our mouths comes from what we believe in our hearts. It is very, very important that we speak words of holiness and not unrighteousness. You are not to curse or say anything foul. You're not to slander and gossip about others.

I know you hear cursing everywhere—on television, in the movies, in places of business, where you work, etc. But that's not how believers are to talk.

But if you listen to it, read it and watch television, movies and other media where people are cursing, and let it into your mind and heart, you'll eventually begin saying it as well. Cursing is a way of life for many, but cursing someone or something is a serious matter. We are blessers, not cursers.

Ephesians 4:29 in *The Amplified Bible, Classic Edition* says, "Let no foul or polluting language, nor evil word nor unwholesome or worthless talk [ever] come out of your mouth, but only such [speech] as is good and beneficial to the spiritual progress of others, as is fitting to the need and the occasion, that it may be a blessing and give grace to those who hear it."

Our words are to minister grace and be a blessing. Foul language doesn't edify people, and it is not beneficial to the spiritual progress of others or yourself.

"But Gloria," you may say, "sometimes I just slip up."

If you slip up and say something that's not right, or you curse, speak a foul word, or speak against someone, repent. Tell the Lord it's not your will and intent to do that. Receive His forgiveness and commit to not say it again.

"Well, what if I slip again sometime later?"

You take the same action again. You repent again. You plead the blood of Jesus over it, and let it cleanse you. Stand against saying those words again. When you think it, rebuke it out of your thoughts. Confess out loud, "That's not part of me anymore. That's my old life. I speak the Word of God. I speak blessings and not cursings. You foul spirit, you foul words, I rebuke you. I break your power in the Name of Jesus. I am a new creature in Christ Jesus. You don't have any authority or any right over me!"

If you'll do that every time you slip or just have negative thoughts, the span of time between slip-ups will grow longer and longer until, one day, you'll be free from the habit of speaking wrong words.

You don't have to curse! You can be free. You can renew your mind and your mouth. Practice it just as you've been learning these past few weeks. You can do it!

STEP OF FAITH:

Ask the Holy Spirit to correct you when you say something foul. Instead, speak holiness—speak what God's Word says about the situation or person.

NOTES

NOTES

NOTES

DAY 16

GIVE THE HOLY SPIRIT SOMETHING TO HELP

"The mind of the wise instructs his mouth, and adds learning and persuasiveness to his lips."

Proverbs 16:23, The Amplified Bible, Classic Edition

God has made mighty provision for your continued success. That's a powerful statement. But it's true. He has given you *much!* He has given you everything you need to succeed in this life. He's given you His Word, the blood of Jesus and the power of the Holy Spirit, just to name some of them.

But for these things to work, you have to do your part. Some people who don't understand this waste a great deal of time. When they find themselves in a hard situation, they often sit back and wait for God to rescue them.

You won't get anywhere by just waiting for God to do everything. As one minister says, "The Holy Spirit is your Helper, and if you don't do what you're supposed to, He doesn't have anything to help."

So, don't just sit there—do something!

Fight the good fight of faith. Put the Word of God in your heart and in your mouth and get aggressive about it. I know it's hard to speak words of faith when you're facing an impossible situation. But you were born again to be able to accomplish hard things!

When Ken and I first began to hear the word of faith, we were in an impossible situation financially. We were so desperate, we *had* to believe God. It was the hardest believing we ever did, too, because we didn't know very much then. But we got aggressive with our faith. We got aggressive with the Word.

The fact is, if you want to lay hold of the authority of God and walk in the supernatural, you aren't going to do it from your spiritual easy chair. You have to press toward it. As Jesus said, "The law and the prophets were until John. Since that time the kingdom of God has been preached, and everyone is pressing into it" (Luke 16:16).

Press. That is such an important word today. If there ever were a generation that needed to press into God, it's ours. So take what God has given you. Get the Word in your heart and in your mouth. Speak it out. Plead the blood of Jesus over your circumstances and your family members. Get aggressive with your faith and give the Holy Spirit something to help!

STEP OF FAITH:

What are you pressing into the Holy Spirit to help you with today? Ask the Holy Spirit to help you, and He will! I believe you will see an immediate change as you press in and ask for His help.

NOTES

NOTES

NOTES

DAY 17

GO AHEAD!
PADDLE UPSTREAM

"Set a guard, O Lord, over my mouth;
keep watch over the door of my lips."

Psalm 141:3

B y now you are probably really understanding the importance of watching over your mouth. You might almost want to say "Ouch," when you hear others say things contrary to the Word. You've become aware of what everyone around you is saying. You have found that most people don't really believe what they say matters. *Even most believers don't believe it.* You can tell that just by listening to their conversations. They profess, for example, to be trusting God concerning their health. But you're likely to hear them say something like this: "I'm just sure I'm going to get the flu. I get it every year. I'll be sicker than a dog, too, you'll see...."

Do people like that have what they say?

Oh, yes! Check with them a few weeks later and they'll be quick to tell you that they got just as sick as they said they'd be. But, odds are, if you were to try to tell them there's any connection between the words they spoke and the illness they suffered, they'd look at you as if you were out of your mind.

Of course, if they would dig into the Word of God and find out what it has to say about the subject, they'd realize that the words they speak have a tremendous impact on their lives. They'd see that it quite literally determines their future. If you've been diligent these past 17 days, you've probably already experienced powerful examples of that. You're finding out firsthand just how powerful your words can be.

Yet, even so, you may still find that speaking faith-filled words consistently is tough to do. It's something you have to watch all the time but eventually it will become your way of life.

You see, the world around you is in a negative flow. Like a rushing river, it's always pulling at you, trying to get you to flow with it. Living by faith and speaking words of faith is like trying to paddle upstream. You can do it—but it takes effort. And there's never a time you can afford to take a vacation from it. All you have to do is relax a little bit and you'll just start drifting right back down the river. You can't afford to drift!

Make the decision right now to set a watch over your lips. Determine to consistently fill your mouth with the Word of God. "My son, give attention to my words; incline your ear to my sayings" (Proverbs 4:20). Let God's Word be the guard over your lips, and everything you say will take you further upstream!

STEP OF FAITH:

Is there something you started working on at the beginning of this book that you've become less diligent about? If so, repent. Turn around and get your words lined up again. Speak the Word to that situation and march forward. Remember, your life is turning around!

NOTES

NOTES

NOTES

DAY 18

SPEAK YOUR HEALING

"My son, attend to my words; consent and submit to my sayings.
Let them not depart from your sight; keep them in the center of
your heart. For they are life to those who find them,
healing and health to all their flesh."

Proverbs 4:20-22, The Amplified Bible, Classic Edition

Have you ever heard someone say, "I'd have no problem at all believing God's Word would heal me if He'd speak to me out loud like He did in Genesis, but He hasn't"?

The answer to that is, "No, and He probably won't either." You see, God no longer has to thunder His Word down at us from heaven. These days He lives in the hearts of believers, so He speaks to us primarily from the inside instead of the outside. What's more, when it comes to covenant issues like healing, we don't even have to wait on Him to speak.

He has already spoken! He has already said, "By whose [Jesus'] stripes you were healed" (1 Peter 2:24). He has already said, "I am the Lord who heals you" (Exodus 15:26). He has already said, "And the prayer of faith will save the sick, and the Lord will raise him up" (James 5:15).

God has already done His part, so we must do ours. We must

take the Word He has spoken, put it inside us and let it change us from the inside out. Everything—including healing—starts inside you. Your future is literally stored up in your heart. That's confirmed in Matthew 12:35: "A good man out of the good treasure of his heart brings forth good things, and an evil man out of the evil treasure brings forth evil things."

In other words, if you want external conditions to be better tomorrow, you'd better start changing your internal condition today. You'd better start depositing the Word of God into your heart. Then when sickness attacks your body, you can tap into the healing Word you've put inside yourself and run that sickness off with your words!

Exactly how do you do that? You open your mouth and *speak*—not words of sickness and disease, discouragement and despair, but words of healing and life, faith and hope. You follow the last step of God's divine prescription in Proverbs 4:20-24: "Put away from you a deceitful mouth, and put perverse lips far from you." In short, you speak the Word of God, and call yourself healed in Jesus' Name.

Despite all you've learned about the power of your words, you may still find this a challenge to do. But you must do it anyway, because for faith to work, it must be in two places—in your heart and in your mouth. "For with the heart one believes unto righteousness, and with the mouth confession is made unto salvation" (Romans 10:10).

So get into the Word. Fill your heart with the good treasure of God's Word for your healing, and speak forth from your heart that Word in faith. Then you'll have your faith in all the right places!

STEP OF FAITH:

When you feel a pain or a symptom, don't let reaching for the medicine cabinet be your *first* reaction. Reach for the Word that is stored up in your heart. Say, "Father, according to 1 Peter 2:24, by Your stripes I am healed. I thank You that I am pain-free and symptom-free in Jesus' Name!" Learn to speak to the situation or thing that you want changed in the Name of Jesus.

NOTES

NOTES

NOTES

DAY 19

SPEAK HIS WORDS ABOUT YOURSELF

"The mind of the wise instructs his mouth, and adds learning and persuasiveness to his lips."

Proverbs 16:23, The Amplified Bible, Classic Edition

Most of us have been naturally trained to speak negatively about ourselves, rather than positively. People do it in the simplest of situations. When they're asked to serve in some capacity, they say, "Oh, I couldn't do that."

When we do that, we step right into the devil's trap. Satan's sole purpose is to deceive and destroy you. He knows there is authority in your words. Since he doesn't have any authority of his own, he deceives you into speaking negatively about yourself, thereby getting you to use your OWN authority against yourself!

If he can just get you to speak harmful things about yourself, he doesn't have to bother with you anymore. If he can get you to speak words against yourself—words of sickness, poverty, being overweight, growing old, having tragedy in your family, never getting that promotion—he knows he has control. And he can go to work on the next person. His practice is teaching people to enforce their own defeat.

He knows you'll get what you say. So if he can train you to say negative things, then that's all he has to do. You keep the door open.

That's how most people have been brought up—to speak negatively against themselves.

As a believer, receive the revelation of the authority you have. Don't let Satan have it. Don't let him have your words.

God's success formula for your life begins with speaking God's Word. Speak the Word that gives you the help you need. Speak the Word of God that gives you the peace you're after. Speak the Word of God that gives you the prosperity you're after. You can speak the Word of God for anything you need.

STEP OF FAITH:

Speak positive things today. Don't put yourself down. Speak the Word of God over yourself. Put your confidence in God and what His Word says about you. Find and study all the scriptures in the Bible about who you are "in Christ" and "in Him." Write them down in a notebook and meditate on them.

Meditating means to:

1. Allow the Holy Spirit to make God's Word a reality in your life.
2. Carefully ponder how this Word applies to your life.
3. Apply it by using it and operating in it.
4. Place yourself in agreement with what God says about you, and speak it aloud. If you see something in the Word that God says you are, then that's what you are. You may not look like it, you may not feel like it. But make yourself agree with the Word in your heart and in your mouth.
5. See yourself as God sees you, and say it!
6. Begin to realize the integrity—the truthfulness—of God's Word.

God's Word is true. It will work. It does not fail. It cannot fail. It is supernatural and has the power in it to bring itself to pass. So, let God's powerful Word renew your mind about what you say about yourself, and dare to believe it!

NOTES

NOTES

NOTES

DAY 20

THE TRAP OF
FLATTERING WORDS

"Let it not even be named among you, as is fitting for saints;
neither filthiness, nor foolish talking, nor coarse jesting, which
are not fitting, but rather giving of thanks."

Ephesians 5:3-4

S atan hasn't come up with any new temptations since the beginning, but he certainly has become more and more bold about them.

Today, you can turn on the television or other electronic devices, and anything you want to watch is available. And everything you see there actually happens. The adultery, the office romances—all of it is very real. It isn't "just on TV" or other media.

Proverbs 2:14-16 says in *The Amplified Bible, Classic Edition:*

Who rejoice to do evil and delight in the perverseness of evil, who are crooked in their ways, wayward and devious in their paths. [Discretion shall watch over you, understanding shall keep you] to deliver you from the alien woman, from the outsider with her flattering words.

These were words to a young prince about marrying a heathen woman, but you could apply them to us today. You could replace the words "alien woman" with "wicked woman" or "wicked man."

If you are married, and some good-looking man or woman comes up to you and starts telling you how wonderful and attractive you are, let discretion rise up within you. Check out of that situation. Don't open your mouth and start speaking and taking part in that temptation. Shut the door to it. Run for your life!

Now, maybe you've been married a while and your spouse doesn't tell you how wonderful you are or how nice you look every morning. Maybe he or she doesn't speak to you at all! But don't fall for the flattery trap at the office.

And don't you be the one who's speaking the flattery either! Watch your words. Don't even let words of lust or flattery open the door to the devil to work in your life.

Proverbs 2 also says in verses 16-21:

> [Discretion shall watch over you, understanding shall keep you] to deliver you from the alien woman, from the outsider with her flattering words, who forsakes the husband and guide of her youth and forgets the covenant of her God. For her house sinks down to death and her paths to the spirits [of the dead]. None who go to her return again, neither do they attain or regain the paths of life. So may you walk in the way of good men, and keep to the paths of the [consistently] righteous (the upright, in right standing with God). For the upright shall dwell in the land, and the men of integrity, blameless and complete [in God's sight], shall remain in it *(The Amplified Bible, Classic Edition)*.

If you've had a habit of telling coarse jokes or saying lustful things to other people, whether it be on the job or elsewhere, stop it now. Turn to the Word and allow it to deliver you and change you. Even if you've never followed through and committed adultery, saying wrong words to men or women, whether you are married or not, is sin.

Repent before God. Ask Him to help you. Study the book of Proverbs. Let God's Word speak to you about your behavior. Don't follow the devil down the path of destruction. Turn your mouth and your heart over to God.

STEP OF FAITH:

Begin today to make a change. When you're tempted to flirt or make remarks, stop yourself. Confess God's Word. Say, "Father, according to Ephesians 5, I will not speak filthiness and coarse jesting. I will not speak lust or open the door to immorality or adultery with my words. I will speak Your Words only. I will speak words of life and goodness in Jesus' Name. Amen."

NOTES

NOTES

NOTES

DAY 21

YOU'RE DOING GREAT—DON'T QUIT

"The tongues of those who are upright and in right standing with God are as choice silver; the minds of those who are wicked and out of harmony with God are of little value."

Proverbs 10:20, The Amplified Bible, Classic Edition

No matter what bait Satan has been throwing at you these past three weeks, remember, he can't force you to do anything. He doesn't have the power. All he can do is make a presentation and try to sell you the lies he's peddling. He can't make you buy them. He can only present them. You have a choice whether to take him up on his sorry deal, or verbally rebuke him and command him to leave you.

So when he makes the next presentation, don't toy with it. Don't take the bait. Instead, immediately turn away from his doubts and start thinking and speaking the Word of God. Ask yourself, *What does the Word say that guarantees me the very thing the devil just tried to make me doubt?*

Always go back to God's Word and find out the real truth. That's where your authority is—in the truth. Satan will lie, cheat, trick, deceive and bait you into bondage—as I'm sure you've experienced. But God will always tell you the truth. And that truth will make you free.

So don't buy his lies. Once you know the truth of your authority in Christ Jesus, you won't spend your days crying about how bad things are. You'll spend your days telling those mountains to be cast into the sea.

Instead of acting like a whiner, you'll be more than a conqueror in Christ. You'll kick the devil out of your affairs with the words of your mouth. And as you stand in triumph with your needs met, your body healed, and your heart rejoicing, you can laugh right in the face of that snake as he slinks away devastated by his defeat.

If you've diligently applied the truths in this book, I know you're doing well. Don't quit. Keep watching your words. You *are* more than a conqueror!

STEP OF FAITH:

Stop right now and assess how far you have come in the past 21 days in changing your life by changing your words. Throw your head back right now and shout in the devil's face: "I am more than a conqueror!"

NOTES

NOTES

NOTES

DAY 22

KEEP YOUR
WORDS IN LINE

*"He who guards his mouth and his tongue
keeps himself from troubles."*

Proverbs 21:23, The Amplified Bible, Classic Edition

There's just no two ways around it. To live a life of blessing, you're going to have to make your words agree with what God says—not just for a few hours or a few days, but all the time.

Since you've worked on this, you know it's not easy. As time wears on and the circumstances around you appear to be stubbornly determined to stay in the same miserable condition they've always been in, it's hard to keep on believing and speaking God's Word. But you have to hold to His Word if you want your harvest of blessing to come in.

When Kenneth started preaching prosperity, I sat out there and listened to him with holes in the bottom of my shoes. We had terrible financial problems. But we knew those problems didn't change what the Word of God said. We knew God's prosperity promises were true even if we hadn't been able to tap into them yet. So, we just kept on talking about God's generous provision for us.

I realized later that the Word went to work for us from the first day we began to believe it, speak it and order our lives according to it. Our prosperity crop began to grow the moment we believed God and started putting seeds into the ground. It just took time for them to come up.

The problem is, most believers don't last that long. They start planting well enough, but then when they don't see immediate results, the bank account is getting low and rent is past due, they get discouraged and begin to speak words of lack and defeat. They tear up their crop with the words of their own mouths, and never get to enjoy the fruit of it.

The next time you strike out in faith, whether it's in the financial realm or any other area, keep that in mind. Determine from the beginning that you're not going to let that waiting period discourage you. Then hang on until the Word of God is manifested in your life. Keep sowing God's promises with your heart and mouth! Put patience to work, and keep your words in line. You *will* receive your harvest.

STEP OF FAITH:

Think about a time when you let your words get out of line with God's Word. What was the result? What would you do now about that situation? What would be the outcome now? If that situation still exists, line your words up and get ready for breakthrough!

NOTES

NOTES

NOTES

DAY 23

TALK TO YOURSELF!

"The mouth of the [uncompromisingly] righteous man is a well of life, but the mouth of the wicked conceals violence."

Proverbs 10:11, The Amplified Bible, Classic Edition

In this day and hour we need to be walking in God's BLESS-ING more than ever. As believers, we need to be walking in our full inheritance, because this age is about to be brought to a close. We have to be alert and awake. It's time we stop allowing the devil to darken our homes, our businesses, our churches and our individual lives with words of strife and envy. It's time we start speaking life and living in the light!

You may be thinking, *I've been working on it, but it's easier said than done!*

I know. But you can do it.

Watch over yourself. Pay attention to your state of mind. When you find yourself depressed or downcast, don't just ignore those feelings. Go to God's Word immediately. Think back. Ask yourself, *What started this downturn?*

You may realize that a particular situation with a co-worker or loved one sparked feelings of aggravation, jealousy or strife within you. If so, look at that situation through the eyes of God, and then talk to it (Mark 11:23).

Say, "That situation has no power over me. I refuse to allow it to bring envy and strife into my life. I yield to the forces of love and joy within me. I am filled to overflowing with the love of God."

Then start praising God. Sing a song. Play a CD or song that will lift you up, and force yourself to sing along. Before long, the love of God will be bubbling up out of your heart again, and you'll be singing from a pure heart.

The coming of Jesus is near at hand. We want Him to find us standing tall in the spirit—full of love, faith and power—walking in the victory Jesus bought for us.

We want Him to find us speaking life and living in the light!

STEP OF FAITH:

Give yourself a little Holy Spirit pep talk right now. Go to the scriptures at the back of this book, and read (or sing) at least 10 of them out loud and see how your thinking changes about yourself and about others!

NOTES

NOTES

NOTES

DAY 24

ANSWER YOUR CIRCUMSTANCES WITH JOY!

"A man has joy by the answer of his mouth...."

Proverbs 15:23

Whatever is happening in your life today, don't let it get you into depression. Stir up the joy that is within you as a born-again child of God.

You can begin by meditating on the Word of God. When you meditate on the Word and revelation begins to rise in your heart, joy comes! It comes because you begin to have a deeper and clearer knowledge of the Father. It comes because you realize you can go boldly before Him in prayer on the basis of the Word, and be confident your prayers will be answered.

If you've been sorrowing over a wayward child, for example, you can replace your sad thoughts with a revelation of God's promise in Isaiah 54:13—"All your children shall be taught by the Lord, and great shall be the peace of your children"—and joy will come into your heart. Stand on that. Say that!

Suddenly, instead of crying over what the devil is doing to

that child, you can start shouting about what God will do. You can laugh and say, "You might as well forget it, devil. Just pack it up and go home right now, because as far as I'm concerned, the victory is won. All my children shall be taught of the Lord. And great shall be the peace of my children!"

Then, when the devil comes back at you and says, *Maybe so, but aren't you sorry over all the years that child has wasted?* you can shoot the Word right back at him. You can say, "No, I'm not sorry. I don't have to be sorry because Jesus bore my griefs and carried my sorrows (Isaiah 53:4). So I believe I'll just go ahead and have myself a grand time rejoicing in Him!"

Proverbs 15:23 says, "A man has joy by the answer of his mouth, and a word spoken in due season, how good it is!" When you start answering the troubles and trials you're facing with the Word of God, it will release joy in you and run the devil off. He can't stand the joy of the Lord!

So stir up that joy within you. Meditate on the Word. Replace wrong thoughts with God's thoughts. And enjoy the victory!

STEP OF FAITH:

What trouble or trial is facing you today? Stir up your joy and run the devil off by rebuking him in the Name of Jesus and speaking God's Word over that situation, right now. Say, "I have the victory over _____." You name the situation and call it done. You believe you receive the victory according to Mark 11:22-24. Then, don't ever say anything to disagree with your faith. If you do, repent and speak God's Word which is the truth about the matter. Then say, "I have received it. Victory is mine now!"

NOTES

NOTES

NOTES

DAY 25

PROTECT YOUR SPIRIT WITH YOUR MOUTH

"The words of a [discreet and wise] man's mouth are like deep waters [plenteous and difficult to fathom], and the fountain of skillful and godly Wisdom is like a gushing stream [sparkling, fresh, pure, and life-giving]."

Proverbs 18:4, The Amplified Bible, Classic Edition

So many people walk around saying things like, "Well, I'm just so tired" or, "I'm so weak" or, "Things are looking so bad." Then, as Ken so aptly puts it, suddenly they think they're going to jerk their faith out from under the table and raise the dead with it.

Well, they'll never be able to do it. Spiritual things don't work that way. Yes, these people need to develop their faith, but not to get out of a crisis and then forget about it until the next crisis. Faith comes by hearing and hearing by the Word of God. You have to keep the Word going into your ears and keep it before your eyes all the time. You have to keep faith active every day so it can stay strong and increase.

According to Proverbs 4:20-21, God says you should keep His Word constantly in your ears and before your eyes so that it gets down into your heart. He says to guard your heart diligently. To be *diligent* means to be "hardworking, industrious, persevering."

Why do you have to be so diligent with the Word? Because the devil is diligent with his lies and deceptions. He's constantly throwing obstacles in your path. He works diligently to make sure the world is surrounding you with fear, sickness, poverty and every other kind of unbelief he can use to destroy you.

But you can protect your spirit from those things by conditioning yourself to respond to every doubt with the Word of God. You've been working daily at this. Don't give up and don't quit. Be diligent about the Word. Be diligent about speaking the Word. Remember, speaking the Word is a part of your daily life. You *can* do it!

STEP OF FAITH:

If someone offends you today, or says something hurtful to you, confess and stand on Psalm 119:165, "Great peace have they who love Your law; nothing shall offend them or make them stumble" *(The Amplified Bible, Classic Edition).*

Pray in your own words like this: "Father, I refuse to be offended. I choose to walk in peace. I forgive them and release them of that offense. I will not be offended. In Jesus' Name."

Now, stand your ground. Don't undo what you've said by saying anything contrary to your confession of faith, even if you feel hurt. Don't let it take root in your heart. Just stand on the Word of truth. Be diligent in protecting your heart.

NOTES

NOTES

NOTES

DAY 26

SHOUT THE VICTORY!

*"Truthful lips shall be established forever, but a lying tongue is
[credited] but for a moment."*

Proverbs 12:19, The Amplified Bible, Classic Edition

Matthew 5:10-12 is the secret to overcoming persecution:
"Blessed are those who are persecuted for righteousness' sake, for theirs is the kingdom of heaven. Blessed
are you when they revile and persecute you, and say all kinds of
evil against you falsely for My sake. Rejoice and be exceedingly
glad, for great is your reward in heaven, for so they persecuted
the prophets who were before you."

At the very moment when persecution comes, you are not
to be depressed—nor are you to let all kinds of fleshly words fly.
You're not to be angry or discouraged. You are to forgive. Then,
rejoice and be glad! Not just glad, but exceedingly glad!

Luke 6:23 takes that command even further. It says, "Rejoice in
that day [of persecution] and leap for joy! For indeed your reward
is great in heaven."

A few days after I first noticed that instruction in the Scripture, someone came into my office and told me of something critical that had been written about us. So I just took that verse literally. I got up and began to leap for joy. "Glory to God! Joy, joy, joy!" I shouted.

I'm sure the person sitting on the other side of my desk was surprised, but I didn't care because the Word worked. I found out you can't jump for joy and shout praises to God and be depressed at the same time.

Remember that the next time persecution comes your way. Remember that the next time a co-worker spreads lies or gossip around about you. It will ruin the devil's whole scheme. He thinks he has figured out what that persecution will do to you. He thinks it will discourage you and stop you in your tracks.

But if you'll immediately begin to leap and jump for joy, if you'll believe what Jesus said and shout, "Praise God, I'm blessed!" the tables will be turned. The devil will end up being the one who's discouraged. He sent that persecution to stop you and to destroy you, not to bless you. Just think how frustrated he'll be!

STEP OF FAITH:

Think of someone who has persecuted you, whom the devil has used to make you feel less than victorious. Now turn the tables on the devil. Shout, "Glory to God! Joy, joy, joy over this situation today and every day!" You have the power in your words to have total peace in the middle of persecution and trouble!

NOTES

NOTES

NOTES

DAY 27

THERE'S A MIRACLE IN YOUR MOUTH

"For with the heart one believes unto righteousness, and with the mouth confession is made unto salvation."

Romans 10:10

D o you need a miracle? Then believe it, confess it and receive it!

"Oh Gloria, I just don't know if I can do that."

Yes, you can! You've already done it once. When you made Jesus the Lord of your life, you believed, confessed and received the greatest miracle in the universe—the miracle of a reborn spirit! Every other miracle you receive will come in exactly the same way.

You start by simply believing what God's Word says concerning your area of need, by letting that Word change your heart and mind.

A lot of people try to skip that step. They try to believe for a miracle without spending enough time in the Word to change their hearts and minds. They just want to confess it with their mouths and have it instantly appear. But that won't happen. It's what we *believe in our hearts* and say with our mouths that we receive.

If you don't have enough faith yet to believe for the miracle you need, then get more faith. Romans 10:17 says, "So then faith comes by hearing, and hearing by the word of God." So start filling your ears and your heart with the Word until faith for your miracle is born.

That's what the woman did who had the issue of blood. She believed in her heart that she would be healed. Then she spoke her faith out loud and acted on it—and she received her miracle!

It wasn't Jesus' decision. He didn't suddenly say, "You know, I think I'll work a miracle for that little lady today." No. *She* made it happen. She used her faith and drew on the power of God. That's why Jesus said, "Daughter, *your* faith has made you well" (Matthew 9:22).

You have that same opportunity. God's power is always present everywhere. Your faith will bring it into your life, body or circumstances. Do what the woman with the issue of blood did. Reach out to Jesus. Believe, confess and receive your miracle today!

STEP OF FAITH:

Think about what area of your life is your biggest faith challenge. Find the promise in God's Word about this area. Believe you receive the answer when you pray. Speak the answer over the situation based on God's Word. Enter into thanksgiving until the situation changes to victory!

NOTES

NOTES

NOTES

DAY 28

THE PRICE OF COMPROMISE

"Set a guard, O Lord, over my mouth;
keep watch over the door of my lips."

Psalm 141:3

C onsider this: If you won't give the devil any place in your
life, he can't do anything to you. That's right. If you won't
speak words of doubt and unbelief, but instead speak
words of faith, he can't sustain an attack.

You see, if you're born again, Satan doesn't have any authority over you. Jesus Christ is your Lord. Satan can't rob you unless
you authorize that robbery yourself! You authorize him by allowing him to have place in your life.

Satan comes to get your words! That's the only way he can
get a foothold. So refuse to speak words contrary to what you
believe. Speak only faith—even under pressure. No matter what
Satan is saying to you in your thoughts, no matter what people
around you are saying, keep agreeing with the Word of God.
Keep saying what God says.

It will be tough sometimes, I know. But you can do it! When

things look hopeless, don't give up and start speaking defeat. Double up on your confession of faith!

Learn to immediately answer every doubt with God's Word. Learn to answer every fear with God's Word. Learn to do combat with the sword of the Spirit (Ephesians 6:17).

Refuse to allow Satan to intimidate you with threats. He can only do what *you* say. He has no authority over you unless you give it to him. If you won't give him any place, he won't be able to carry out even one of those threats. It's when you become negative, timid and fearful with the words of your mouth that Satan gains the upper hand.

Don't ever allow fear to make you compromise your confession of faith. I learned this long ago: What you compromise to keep, you lose. Stand firm and keep talking faith and you'll defeat any attack.

STEP OF FAITH:

Get ready for the next attack *now!* God's Word covers every area of life. Have His promises in your mouth and at your side constantly. When the attack comes, grab the Word and fight back in faith! Soon God's Word will become so strong in your heart and mind they will flow out of you automatically. Stand your ground and defeat the enemy with the Word!

NOTES

NOTES

NOTES

DAY 29

SPEAK HIS WORDS DAY AND NIGHT

"Your word I have hidden in my heart...."

Psalm 119:11

Whatever you do in life, whether you're a surgeon, a garbage collector or a schoolteacher, spending time with God and keeping your heart full of His Word is your No. 1 priority.

That's right. The most important thing you'll do each day is to make those faith deposits. Don't just make them in times of crisis, either. Make them before you need them. Go to Psalm 91 and proclaim the things that belong to you by faith every day.

I remember a letter Ken and I received from a family whose child drowned in their swimming pool. When they came out and found the baby in the pool, he had already turned blue and was motionless.

But because they had made deposits of the Word of God before that time, the moment it happened, they were ready. No one said, "Go get the Bible and let's look up a scripture." (Sometimes you don't have time to get your Bible. That's why you'd better get the Word into your heart. It will save your life.)

Immediately, that family began to pray and rebuke death and command the spirit of that baby to come back. In other words, they instantly began to *speak* the Word of God, which is full of life and power, to the situation. As a result, that child is alive and well today.

You can have that same kind of faith and Word stored up in your heart, ready to come out of your mouth anytime. All you have to do is continue making deposits of God's Word into your heart every day.

Continue, as you've been practicing these past few weeks, speaking the Word day and night. Don't just do it when you're praying or being spiritual, but all the time—at the office, at the dinner table, over your coffee break, even in your bed at night. The words you speak will either work for you or against you. They are either words of faith or words of doubt.

It's time we turn our attention to filling our hearts with God's Word. We need to become spiritual powerhouses, with hearts so full of faith that we defeat the devil's every scheme.

If we'll do that, we will be able to buy back every piece of ground he's ever stolen from us. We can enjoy the riches of our inheritance at last!

STEP OF FAITH:

Sit down today and develop a personal plan to make a deposit of God's Word into your heart every day. Read His Word, believe it, speak it, act on it, and receive what it promises. That's the process of living the life of faith—the life of victory!

NOTES

NOTES

NOTES

DAY 30

GIVE YOURSELF
A NEW NAME

*"All the words of my mouth are righteous (upright and in right
standing with God); there is nothing contrary
to truth or crooked in them."*

Proverbs 8:8, The Amplified Bible, Classic Edition

People can read the Bible, they can even memorize it, and
still live totally in unbelief. They can do this because they
don't *apply* the Word. They're just reading it. They haven't
received any revelation from the Spirit of God about what they're
reading. Therefore, it isn't in their hearts, and they aren't speaking
it out of their mouths and acting on it in faith.

Now, some people can't believe that this could be right. They
also don't believe that what they say every day is really all that
important. But your words form your future. The words you speak
all the time, not just in prayer, are your faith speaking. That's
what's in your heart (Luke 6:45).

You can be a believer and walk by faith, but when you quit
feeding on the Word, you'll soon begin speaking wrong words.
You'll start talking words of defeat and doubt, speaking the

problem, focusing on the sickness and disease, giving attention to the part of the curse that's trying to come into your life. (You can read about the curse in Deuteronomy 28.)

Have you ever noticed that when you experience symptoms in your body, you just feel like you have to tell someone? Well, the next time that happens, do yourself a favor and don't!

We're all guilty of this. I've done it. One time, I hurt my finger. I just wanted to talk about that little finger. I found myself telling Ken, "My finger hurts so bad." And then I realized what I was doing!

When you find yourself speaking words of pain instead of words of healing—get right back into the Word and put what God says about it in your mouth. Get right back in faith.

You wouldn't think that words could take you from a place of defeat and put you over into total victory. But they can. When you let God's words become your words, supernatural things happen. God's Word is supernatural. It has the power to bring itself to pass.

When we dwell on and meditate on the Word of God and the truth that our heavenly Father loves us, that we've been redeemed from sickness, disease and poverty, that our seed is blessed, and that we're to live in victory, then our thinking begins to straighten out and get in agreement with God.

First John 5:5 says, "Who is he who overcomes the world, but he who believes that Jesus is the Son of God?"

When we get our words in line with what God says, then we can have victory that overcomes the world. When we get our words in line with what we're believing for, it will come to pass. If you're believing to be out of debt and your bills paid, for example, then give yourself a new name. Call yourself John Prosperous Smith today, or Mary Abounding Taylor. I know that sounds funny, but do it anyway. Call yourself what you want to come to pass. Activate your faith—speak it!

STEP OF FAITH:

Purpose in your heart today that you will stay in God's Word continually. Find out who you really are in Him. Take steps of faith to become all His Word says about you. Call yourself who God says you are and confess what He says you can do!

NOTES

NOTES

NOTES

DAY 31

IN THE LONG RUN...

"By long forbearance and calmness of spirit a judge or ruler is persuaded, and soft speech breaks down the most bonelike resistance."

Proverbs 25:15, The Amplified Bible, Classic Edition

Ken and I have studied faith, healing, prosperity and many other truths in God's Word for many, many years. Third John 2 says, "Beloved, I pray that you may prosper in all things and be in health, just as your soul prospers." So for you to prosper in other areas of your life, you'll have to have a prosperous soul. Through all these years of study, one truth stands out: What we know doesn't get us delivered. But rather, it's the continual, daily feeding of our spirit man with the Word that delivers, changes and speaks to us. It's what we say from a heart full of faith and act on that determines our future.

As I've said throughout this book, when the Word of God lives in our spirit man (our hearts) and comes out of our mouths to be applied to circumstances and situations, it has in it the creative power of God to bring itself to pass. God's Word *is* His creative power. And He's given us the privilege of being a depository for

His supernatural Word that is "energizing, and effective," as the *Amplified Bible, Classic Edition,* says in Hebrews 4:12.

When His Word is in your heart, it is abiding in there full of its supernatural power. Then, when you release it through speaking it in faith, its creative, energizing power applied to your circumstances begins to change them. It's so simple. God's Word is alive!

So keep that Word fresh and alive in you. You've learned much in 31 days. Keep yourself stirred up. Keep yourself listening to what comes out of your mouth. Whatever it is you still hear yourself saying that is contrary to God's Word and His ways, center your focus on that today. Don't give up. Double up on your confession of the Word. Write it on index cards and carry them with you. Practice, practice, practice. Your diligence and faithfulness will be rewarded (Hebrews 11:6). If you'll stay with it and don't give up, you *will* have what you say!

STEP OF FAITH:

Always remember, as I learned in my early days of faith: *In consistency lies the power.* Be diligent with God's Word to (1) hear it, (2) believe it, (3) speak it, (4) act on it and finally, (5) expect it to come to pass! Think about Mark 11:23. Jesus said to *believe what you say, and it shall come to pass.* When you change your words, you'll change your life—and change your world!

NOTES

NOTES

NOTES

HOW'S YOUR HABIT?

YOU MADE IT! IT'S BEEN 31 DAYS. So how's your habit? Have you noticed a difference? Have your family members or co-workers noticed a difference? The key to your continual success is faithfulness and diligence.

For example, have you ever noticed that those who have the most exciting, faith-inspiring testimonies are those who've been under pressure at some time in their lives? They're the people who stayed faithful when the pressure was on—people who believed God's promises of prosperity in the midst of desperate financial situations, or who trusted God for healing in the face of a terminal disease.

When you get into a hard spot is not the time to back out on God and re-evaluate His faithfulness.

When tough times keep dragging on and the situations around you seem to refuse to get in line with the promises of God, don't re-evaluate God! He's not missing it, and He's not failing.

If you're going to re-evaluate anything, re-evaluate yourself! Look and see where you may have failed. If you still can't find out what the problem is, just say, "God, I don't know what's wrong here, and I'm asking You to show me. But one thing I know, the problem is not with You, and I continue to be moved only by what Your Word says and not by my circumstances." Then, when He reveals something to you about it, be quick to make changes.

I want to encourage you to stand firm and to keep honoring God with your words. The Lord is listening to you when the pressure is on (Malachi 3:16). Let Him hear your words of faith, healing, prosperity, goodness, love and giving. Let Him hear words of life!

Keep *speaking* right words. Keep speaking the Word of God to your circumstances. Go back to the beginning of this book and start reading it again. Meditate on each day's encouragement. Your very life—your future—is in your mouth. Make it full of the life of God!

Gloria

RENEW YOUR MIND...
AND YOUR MOUTH!

Scriptures to Live By

(DEUTERONOMY 6:5-7)

You shall love the Lord your God with all your heart, with all
your soul, and with all your strength. And these words which I
command you today shall be in your heart. You shall teach them
diligently to your children, and shall **talk** of them when you sit in
your house, when you walk by the way, when you lie down, and
when you rise up.

(DEUTERONOMY 11:18-20)

Therefore you shall lay up these words of mine in your heart and
in your soul, and bind them as a sign on your hand, and they
shall be as frontlets between your eyes. You shall teach them to
your children, **speaking** of them when you sit in your house,
when you walk by the way, when you lie down, and when you
rise up. And you shall write them on the doorposts of your house
and on your gates.

(JOSHUA 1:8)

This Book of the Law shall not depart from your **mouth,** but you
shall meditate in it day and night, that you may observe to do
according to all that is written in it. For then you will make your
way prosperous, and then you will have good success.

(PSALM 103:5)

[God] satisfies your **mouth** with good things, so that your youth is renewed like the eagle's.

(PSALM 119:46)

I will **speak** of Your testimonies also before kings, and will not be ashamed.

(PSALM 141:3)

Set a guard, O Lord, over my **mouth;** keep watch over the door of my lips.

(PROVERBS 4:20-21, 23)

My son, give attention to my **words;** incline your ear to my sayings. Do not let them depart from your eyes; keep them in the midst of your heart.... Keep your heart with all diligence, for out of it spring the issues of life.

(PROVERBS 4:24, *The Amplified Bible, Classic Edition*)

Put away from you false and dishonest **speech,** and willful and contrary **talk** put far from you.

(PROVERBS 6:2, *The Amplified Bible, Classic Edition*)

You are snared with the words of your lips, you are caught by the **speech** of your **mouth.**

(PROVERBS 8:7, *The Amplified Bible, Classic Edition*)
For my **mouth** shall **utter** truth, and wrongdoing is detestable and loathsome to my lips.

(PROVERBS 8:8, *The Amplified Bible, Classic Edition*)
All the words of my **mouth** are righteous (upright and in right standing with God); there is nothing contrary to truth or crooked in them.

(PROVERBS 8:13, *The Amplified Bible, Classic Edition*)
The reverent fear and worshipful awe of the Lord [includes] the hatred of evil; pride, arrogance, the evil way, and perverted and twisted **speech** I hate.

(PROVERBS 10:11, *The Amplified Bible, Classic Edition*)
The **mouth** of the [uncompromisingly] righteous man is a well of life, but the **mouth** of the wicked conceals violence.

(PROVERBS 10:13, *The Amplified Bible, Classic Edition*)
On the **lips** of him who has discernment, skillful and godly Wisdom is found, but discipline and the rod are for the back of him who is without sense and understanding.

(PROVERBS 10:14, *The Amplified Bible, Classic Edition*)
Wise men store up knowledge [in mind and heart], but the **mouth** of the foolish is a present destruction.

(PROVERBS 10:19, *The Amplified Bible, Classic Edition*)
In a multitude of **words** transgression is not lacking, but he who restrains his lips is prudent.

(PROVERBS 10:20, *The Amplified Bible, Classic Edition*)
The **tongues** of those who are upright and in right standing with God are as choice silver; the mind of those who are wicked and out of harmony with God are of little value.

(PROVERBS 10:21, *The Amplified Bible, Classic Edition*)
The **lips** of the [uncompromisingly] righteous feed and guide many, but fools die for want of understanding and heart.

(PROVERBS 10:31, *The Amplified Bible, Classic Edition*)
The **mouths** of the righteous (those harmonious with God) bring forth skillful and godly Wisdom, but the perverse tongue shall be cut down [like a barren and rotten tree].

(PROVERBS 10:32, *The Amplified Bible, Classic Edition*)
The lips of the [uncompromisingly] righteous know [and therefore utter] what is acceptable, but the mouth of the wicked knows [and therefore **speaks** only] what is obstinately willful and contrary.

(PROVERBS 11:9, *The Amplified Bible, Classic Edition*)
With his **mouth** the godless man destroys his neighbor, but through knowledge and superior discernment shall the righteous be delivered.

(PROVERBS 11:11, *The Amplified Bible, Classic Edition*)
By the blessing of the influence of the upright and God's favor
[because of them] the city is exalted, but it is overthrown by the
mouth of the wicked.

(PROVERBS 11:12, *The Amplified Bible, Classic Edition*)
He who **belittles** and despises his neighbor lacks sense, but a
man of understanding keeps silent.

(PROVERBS 12:13)
The wicked is ensnared by the transgression of his **lips,** but the
righteous will come through trouble.

(PROVERBS 12:14)
A man will be satisfied with good by the fruit of his **mouth,** and
the recompense of a man's hands will be rendered to him.

(PROVERBS 12:18, *The Amplified Bible, Classic Edition*)
There are those who **speak** rashly, like the piercing of a sword,
but the tongue of the wise brings healing.

(PROVERBS 12:19, *The Amplified Bible, Classic Edition*)
Truthful lips shall be established forever, but a **lying tongue** is
[credited] but for a moment.

(PROVERBS 12:22, *The Amplified Bible, Classic Edition*)
Lying lips are extremely disgusting and hateful to the Lord, but
they who deal faithfully are His delight.

(PROVERBS 13:2, *The Amplified Bible, Classic Edition*)
A good man eats good from the fruit of his **mouth,** but the desire of the treacherous is for violence.

(PROVERBS 13:3, *The Amplified Bible, Classic Edition*)
He who guards his **mouth** keeps his life, but he who opens wide his lips comes to ruin.

(PROVERBS 15:2, *The Amplified Bible, Classic Edition*)
The **tongue** of the wise utters knowledge rightly, but the mouth of the [self-confident] fool pours out folly.

(PROVERBS 15:4, *The Amplified Bible, Classic Edition*)
A **gentle tongue** [with its healing power] is a tree of life, but willful contrariness in it breaks down the spirit.

(PROVERBS 15:7, *The Amplified Bible, Classic Edition*)
The lips of the wise **disperse** knowledge [sifting it as chaff from the grain]; not so the minds and hearts of the self-confident and foolish.

(PROVERBS 15:23, *The Amplified Bible, Classic Edition*)
A man has joy in making an apt **answer,** and a word **spoken** at the right moment—how good it is!

(PROVERBS 15:28, *The Amplified Bible, Classic Edition*)
The mind of the [uncompromisingly] righteous studies how to **answer,** but the mouth of the wicked pours out evil things.

(PROVERBS 16:1, *The Amplified Bible, Classic Edition*)
The plans of the mind and orderly thinking belong to man, but
from the Lord comes the [wise] **answer** of the tongue.

(PROVERBS 16:13, *The Amplified Bible, Classic Edition*)
Right and just lips are the delight of a king, and he loves him who
speaks what is right.

(PROVERBS 16:23, *The Amplified Bible, Classic Edition*)
The mind of the wise **instructs his mouth,** and adds learning
and persuasiveness to his lips.

(PROVERBS 16:24, *The Amplified Bible, Classic Edition*)
Pleasant **words** are as a honeycomb, sweet to the mind and healing to the body.

(PROVERBS 16:30, *The Amplified Bible, Classic Edition*)
He who shuts his eyes to devise perverse things and who com-
presses his **lips** [as if in concealment] brings evil to pass.

(PROVERBS 17:7, *The Amplified Bible, Classic Edition*)
Fine or arrogant **speech** does not befit [an empty-headed] fool—
much less do lying lips befit a prince.

(PROVERBS 17:20, *The Amplified Bible, Classic Edition*)
He who has a wayward and crooked mind finds no good, and he
who has a willful and **contrary tongue** will fall into calamity.

(PROVERBS 18:2, *The Amplified Bible, Classic Edition*)
A [self-confident] fool has no delight in understanding but only in revealing his personal **opinions** and himself.

(PROVERBS 18:4, *The Amplified Bible, Classic Edition*)
The **words** of a [discreet and wise] man's mouth are like deep waters [plenteous and difficult to fathom], and the fountain of skillful and godly Wisdom is like a gushing stream [sparkling, fresh, pure, and life-giving].

(PROVERBS 18:6, *The Amplified Bible, Classic Edition*)
A [self-confident] fool's lips bring contention, and his **mouth** invites a beating.

(PROVERBS 18:7, *The Amplified Bible, Classic Edition*)
A [self-confident] fool's **mouth** is his ruin, and his lips are a snare to himself.

(PROVERBS 18:8, *The Amplified Bible, Classic Edition*)
The words of a whisperer or **talebearer** are as dainty morsels; they go down into the innermost parts of the body.

(PROVERBS 18:21, *The Amplified Bible, Classic Edition*)
Death and life are in the power of the **tongue,** and they who indulge in it shall eat the fruit of it [for death or life].

(PROVERBS 19:1, *The Amplified Bible, Classic Edition*)
Better is a poor man who walks in his integrity than a rich man who is perverse in his **speech** and is a [self-confident] fool.

(PROVERBS 19:9, *The Amplified Bible, Classic Edition*)
A false witness shall not be unpunished, and he who **breathes forth** lies shall perish.

(PROVERBS 20:15, *The Amplified Bible, Classic Edition*)
There is gold, and a multitude of pearls; but the **lips** of knowledge are a vase of preciousness [the most precious of all].

(PROVERBS 20:19, *The Amplified Bible, Classic Edition*)
He who goes about as a **talebearer** reveals secrets; therefore associate not with him who talks too freely.

(PROVERBS 21:23, *The Amplified Bible, Classic Edition*)
He who guards his **mouth** and his tongue keeps himself from troubles.

(PROVERBS 22:13, *The Amplified Bible, Classic Edition*)
The sluggard **says,** There is a lion outside! I shall be slain in the streets!

(PROVERBS 22:17-18, *The Amplified Bible, Classic Edition*)
Listen (consent and submit) to the words of the wise, and apply your mind to my knowledge; for it will be pleasant if you keep them in your mind [believing them]; your lips will be accustomed to **[confessing]** them.

(PROVERBS 25:9, *The Amplified Bible, Classic Edition*)
Argue your cause with your neighbor himself; discover not and disclose not another's secret.

(PROVERBS 25:11, *The Amplified Bible, Classic Edition*)
A word fitly **spoken** and in due season is like apples of gold in settings of silver.

(PROVERBS 25:15, *The Amplified Bible, Classic Edition*)
By long forbearance and calmness of spirit a judge or ruler is persuaded, and soft **speech** breaks down the most bonelike resistance.

(PROVERBS 25:23, *The Amplified Bible, Classic Edition*)
The north wind brings forth rain; so does a **backbiting tongue** bring forth an angry countenance.

(PROVERBS 26:28, *The Amplified Bible, Classic Edition*)
A **lying tongue** hates those it wounds and crushes, and a flattering mouth works ruin.

(PROVERBS 29:11, *The Amplified Bible, Classic Edition*)
A [self-confident] fool **utters** all his anger, but a wise man holds it back and stills it.

(PROVERBS 31:26, *The Amplified Bible, Classic Edition*)
She **opens her mouth** in skillful and godly Wisdom, and on her tongue is the law of kindness [giving counsel and instruction].

(PROVERBS 31:27, *The Amplified Bible, Classic Edition*)
She looks well to how things go in her household, and the bread of idleness **(gossip,** discontent, and self-pity) she will not eat.

(ISAIAH 45:19)

I, the Lord, **speak** righteousness, I declare things that are right.

(ISAIAH 54:17)

"No weapon formed against you shall prosper, and every **tongue** which rises against you in judgment you shall condemn. This is the heritage of the servants of the Lord, and their righteousness is from Me," says the Lord.

(ISAIAH 55:11-12)

So shall My word be that goes forth from My **mouth;** it shall not return to Me void, but it shall accomplish what I please, and it shall prosper in the thing for which I sent it. For you shall go out with joy, and be led out with peace; the mountains and the hills shall break forth into singing before you, and all the trees of the field shall clap their hands.

(JEREMIAH 1:9)

Then the Lord put forth His hand and touched my mouth, and the Lord said to me: "Behold, I have put My words in your **mouth."**

(MATTHEW 12:34-37)

For out of the abundance of the heart the mouth **speaks.** A good man out of the good treasure of his heart brings forth good things, and an evil man out of the evil treasure brings forth evil things. But I say to you that for every idle word men may **speak,** they will give account of it in the day of judgment. For by your words you will be justified, and by your words you will be condemned.

(MARK 11:14, 20)

In response Jesus **said** to [the fig tree], "Let no one eat fruit from you ever again." And His disciples **heard** it.... Now in the morning, as they passed by, they saw the fig tree dried up from the roots.

(MARK 11:23)

Whoever **says** to this mountain, "Be removed and be cast into the sea," and does not doubt in his heart, but believes that those things he says will be done, he will have whatever he says.

(MARK 11:24)

Therefore I say to you, whatever things you ask when you **pray,** believe that you receive them, and you will have them.

(ROMANS 4:17)

God...**calls** those things which do not exist as though they did.

(ROMANS 10:10)

For with the heart one believes unto righteousness, and with the **mouth confession** is made unto salvation.

(2 CORINTHIANS 4:13)

I believed and therefore I **spoke....**

(EPHESIANS 4:29)

Let no corrupt **word** proceed out of your **mouth,** but what is good for necessary edification, that it may impart grace to the hearers.

(EPHESIANS 5:3-4)

...let it not even be named among you, as is fitting for saints; neither filthiness, nor foolish **talking,** nor coarse jesting, which are not fitting, but rather giving of thanks.

(HEBREWS 4:12)

The **word of God** is living and powerful, and sharper than any two-edged sword, piercing even to the division of soul and spirit, and of joints and marrow.

(JAMES 1:26)

If anyone among you thinks he is religious, and does not bridle his **tongue** but deceives his own heart, this one's religion is useless.

(JAMES 3:2)

For we all stumble in many things. If anyone does not stumble in **word,** he is a perfect man, able also to bridle the whole body.

(JAMES 3:5-6)

Even so the **tongue** is a little member and boasts great things. See how great a forest a little fire kindles! And the **tongue** is a fire, a world of iniquity. The **tongue** is so set among our members that it defiles the whole body, and sets on fire the course of nature; and it is set on fire by hell.

(JAMES 3:8-12)

But no man can tame the **tongue.** It is an unruly evil, full of deadly poison. With it we bless our God and Father, and with it we curse men, who have been made in the similitude of God. Out of the same **mouth** proceed blessing and cursing. My brethren, these things ought not to be so. Does a spring send forth fresh water and bitter from the same opening? Can a fig tree, my brethren, bear olives, or a grapevine bear figs? Thus no spring yields both salt water and fresh.

Prayer for Salvation and Baptism in the Holy Spirit

Heavenly Father, I come to You in the Name of Jesus. Your Word says, "Whosoever shall call on the name of the Lord shall be saved" (Acts 2:21). I am calling on You. I pray and ask Jesus to come into my heart and be Lord over my life according to Romans 10:9-10: "If thou shalt confess with thy mouth the Lord Jesus, and shalt believe in thine heart that God hath raised him from the dead, thou shalt be saved. For with the heart man believeth unto righteousness; and with the mouth confession is made unto salvation." I do that now. I confess that Jesus is Lord, and I believe in my heart that God raised Him from the dead. I repent of sin. I renounce it. I renounce the devil and everything he stands for. Jesus is my Lord.

I am now reborn! I am a Christian—a child of Almighty God! I am saved! You also said in Your Word, "If ye then, being evil, know how to give good gifts unto your children: HOW MUCH MORE shall your heavenly Father give the Holy Spirit to them that ask him?" (Luke 11:13). I'm also asking You to fill me with the Holy Spirit. Holy Spirit, rise up within me as I praise God. I fully expect to speak with other tongues as You give me the utterance (Acts 2:4). In Jesus' Name. Amen!

Begin to praise God for filling you with the Holy Spirit. Speak those words and syllables you receive—not in your own language, but the language given to you by the Holy Spirit. You have to use your own voice. God will not force you to speak. Don't be concerned with how it sounds. It is a heavenly language!

Continue with the blessing God has given you and pray in the spirit every day.

You are a born-again, Spirit-filled believer. You'll never be the same!

Find a good church that boldly preaches God's Word and obeys it. Become part of a church family who will love and care for you as you love and care for them.

We need to be connected to each other. It increases our strength in God. It's God's plan for us.

Make it a habit to watch the Believer's Voice of Victory Network and become a doer of the Word, who is blessed in his doing (James 1:22-25).

About the Author

Gloria Copeland is a noted author and minister of the gospel whose teaching ministry is known throughout the world. Believers worldwide know her through Believers' Conventions, Victory Campaigns, magazine articles, teaching audios and videos, and the daily and Sunday *Believer's Voice of Victory* television broadcast, which she hosts with her husband, Kenneth Copeland. She is known for Healing School, which she began teaching and hosting in 1979 at KCM meetings. Gloria delivers the Word of God and the keys to victorious Christian living to millions of people every year.

Gloria is author of the New York Times best-seller, *God's Master Plan for Your Life* and *Live Long, Finish Strong,* as well as numerous other favorites, including *God's Will for You, Walk With God, God's Will Is Prosperity, Hidden Treasures* and *To Know Him.* She has also co-authored several books with her husband, including *Family Promises, Healing Promises* and the best-selling daily devotionals, *From Faith to Faith* and *Pursuit of His Presence.*

She holds an honorary doctorate from Oral Roberts University. In 1994, Gloria was voted Christian Woman of the Year, an honor conferred on women whose example demonstrates outstanding Christian leadership. Gloria is also the co-founder and vice president of Kenneth Copeland Ministries in Fort Worth, Texas.

Learn more about Kenneth Copeland Ministries
by visiting our website at **kcm.org**

Materials to Help You Receive Your Healing
by Gloria Copeland

Books
* And Jesus Healed Them All
* God's Prescription for Divine Health
* God's Will for Your Healing
* Harvest of Health

  Words That Heal (gift book with CD enclosed)

Audio Resources
Be Made Whole—Live Long, Live Healthy

God Is a Good God

God Wants You Well

Healing Confessions (CD and minibook)

Healing School

DVD Resources
Be Made Whole—Live Long, Live Healthy

Know Him As Healer

*Available in Spanish

When The LORD first spoke to Kenneth and Gloria Copeland about starting the *Believer's Voice of Victory* magazine...

He said: *This is your seed. Give it to everyone who ever responds to your ministry, and don't ever allow anyone to pay for a subscription!*

For more than 50 years, it has been the joy of Kenneth Copeland Ministries to bring the good news to believers. Readers enjoy teaching from ministers who write from lives of living contact with God, and testimonies from believers experiencing victory through God's WORD in their everyday lives.

Today, the *BVOV* magazine is mailed monthly, bringing encouragement and blessing to believers around the world. Many even use it as a ministry tool, passing it on to others who desire to know Jesus and grow in their faith!

Request your FREE subscription to the *Believer's Voice of Victory* magazine today!

Go to **freevictory.com** to subscribe online, or call us at **1-800-600-7395** (U.S. only) or **+1-817-852-6000**.

We're Here for You!®

Your growth in God's WORD and victory in Jesus are at the very center of our hearts. In every way God has equipped us, we will help you deal with the issues facing you, so you can be the **victorious overcomer** He has planned for you to be.

The mission of Kenneth Copeland Ministries is about all of us growing and going together. Our prayer is that you will take full advantage of all The LORD has given us to share with you.

Wherever you are in the world, you can watch the *Believer's Voice of Victory* broadcast on television (check your local listings), the Internet at kcm.org or on our digital Roku channel.

Our website, **kcm.org,** gives you access to every resource we've developed for your victory. And, you can find contact information for our international offices in Africa, Australia, Canada, Europe, Ukraine and our headquarters in the United States.

Each office is staffed with devoted men and women, ready to serve and pray with you. You can contact the worldwide office nearest you for assistance, and you can call us for prayer at our U.S. number, +1-817-852-6000, 24 hours every day!

We encourage you to connect with us often and let us be part of your everyday walk of faith!

Jesus Is LORD!

Kenneth & Gloria Copeland

Kenneth and Gloria Copeland